HOT CLUB SESSION

BASIC ACOUSTIC SWING JAZZ GUITAR

Swing-Jazz BY FELIX SCHELL

Online Audio www.melbay.com/20819BCDEB

Audio Contents

I0806897

1 2 3 4 5 6 7 8 9 0

Table of Contents

Preface

The Hot Swing Guitar Style has a special stamping. On one hand, it is powerful and vigorous, on the other hand it is humorous and poetic.

The guitar players in those days did not have pick-up systems or the comfort of amplified electric guitars with thin strings and low action. Thus brilliance and sound intensity had to be physically produced. So technological development is partly to blame that so few musicians today know how to play in the original style. Nevertheless the popularity for this music has lasted.

The most important pioneers of the Acoustic Jazz Guitar were Eddie Lang, Django Reinhardt and Oscar Alleman. The tradition went on with "Sinti and Roma" and was formally known as "Gypsy Jazz Guitar" (Häns'sche Weiss Quintet, Schnuckenack Reinhardt Quintet, Birelli Lagrène.)

The title of this book "Hot Club Session" refers to a Jazz Club in Paris named "Hot Club de France". There, the Hot Club Quintet often performed. The Quintet was founded in the thirties by Stephan Grappelli and Django Reinhardt, the guitar player and one of the most important European jazz musicians in history. The fabulous music of this ensemble has been documented on many recordings.

Hot Club Jazz is a European style of jazz music dominated by string instruments. The typical Quintet consists of three guitars, a violin and upright bass. Trumpet, drums or saxophone, associated with traditional American Jazz, are rare.

This edition is designed for guitar players who want to familiarize themselves with the basics of the Acoustic Swing Jazz Style.

Good luck, have fun and enjoy,

Felix Schell

ONE NOTE RHYTHM (1)

One Note Rhythm is based on the Rhythm Changes Form, a form of 32 bars with an AABA structure. The piece begins with a 4 bar intro. Many compositions developed in the swing era were based on this pattern. In this piece, direct your attention to the downstroke and upstroke technique. It is indicated by (⊓) for down stroke and (V) for upstroke. You get the typical sound if you keep the fret hand moving. Experiment with the pressure of your fingers. Keep the pressure, if you want to play legato (holding tone,) remove the pressure suddenly for a staccato sound. Play the single-note lines with the right hand in a relaxed way. Do not hang too close to the bridge with your right hand.

2,13

Felix Schell

B7
7fr.
E7
5fr.
V
(1,2) (3) 4 1 (2) + 3,4
Bridge:
A7
5fr.
D7
3fr.
VII
G6
G♯°7
3fr.
Am7
5fr.
D7
3fr.
IV
Theme:
V

ONE NOTE RHYTHM (2)

Practice the following theme until you find it easy. Pay attention to the first four tones. The fingertips of your left hand may only contact with the strings during the moment of sounding. Left- and right hand act in synchronous. The next tone, (b flat) slides to a and is followed by two staccato tones (G/E).

3,13

Felix Schell

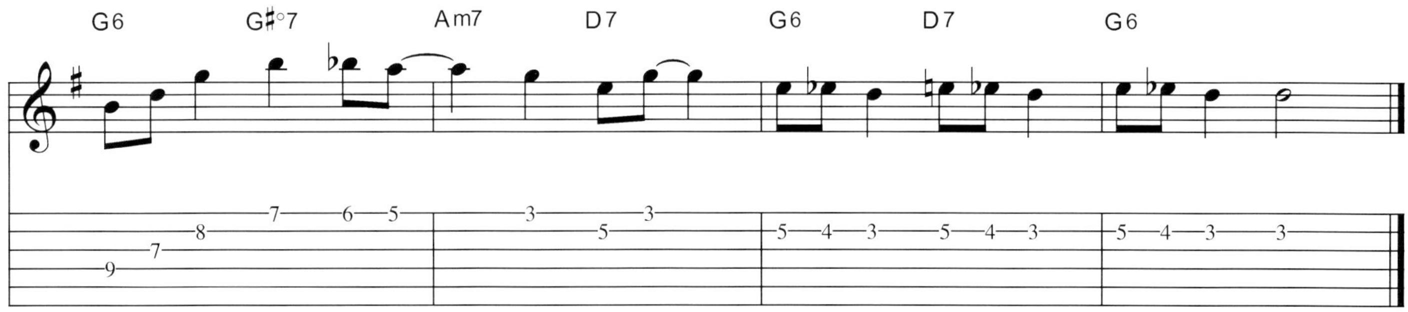

Improvisation tools:

1. Use only the tones of the G major chord (G,B,D) during the A parts (the first 16 bars and the last 8 bars). Although the bars change, it sounds right.

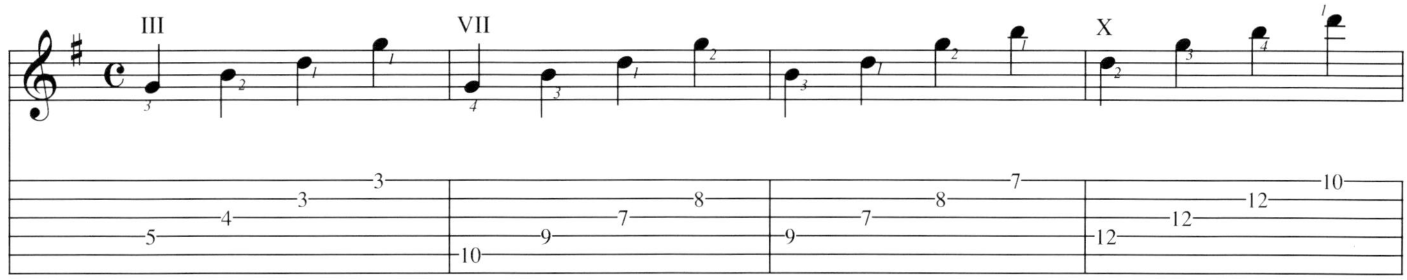

2. Use the tones of the corresponding dominant seven chords in the middle part.

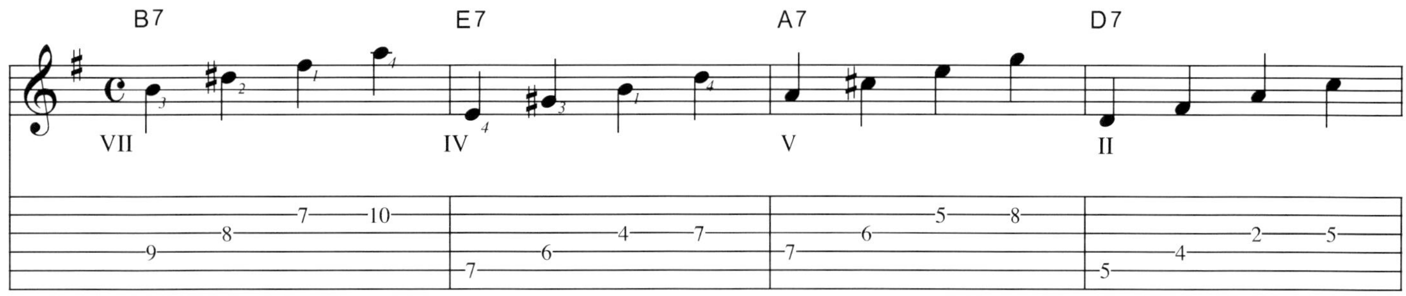

3. Now start playing your own solo.

ONE NOTE RHYTHM (3)

A solo may be interesting, even if it just consists of a few tones. The rhythmic component plays an important role. The following example uses the scheme of 3 over 4. The rhythmic figure repeats itself every third beat. Playing 3 over 4 creates a swinging drive.

4,13

Syncopations in the melodic line are characteristic for jazz music. It is very important to be serious about the rhythm. Clap the rhythm of the melodic line before you start to play. Tap out the basic beat with your feet.

Improvisation tools:

1. For the A-parts, vary the chord tones of G6 (bar 1,3,5,7) and D7 (2,4,6,8).

2. In part B, use the chord tones of B7 for the B7 chord, but then change to the chord tones of Bm6 for the following E7 chord. According to that scheme, keep the tones for A7 but replace the chord tones D7 with the ones of Am6.

MINOR STOMP (1)

Minor stomp has an AABA form in a minor tonality.

Minor Stomp - the chords:

5,14

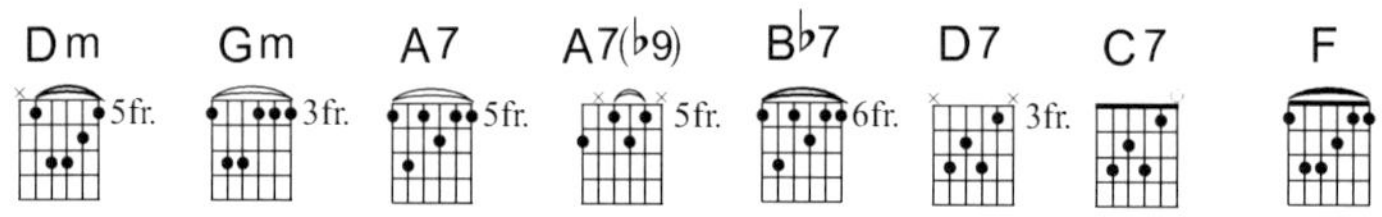

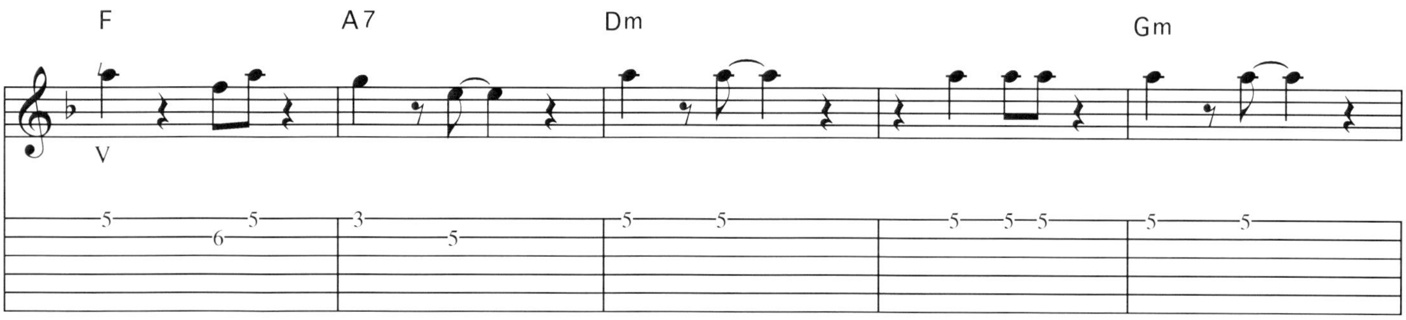

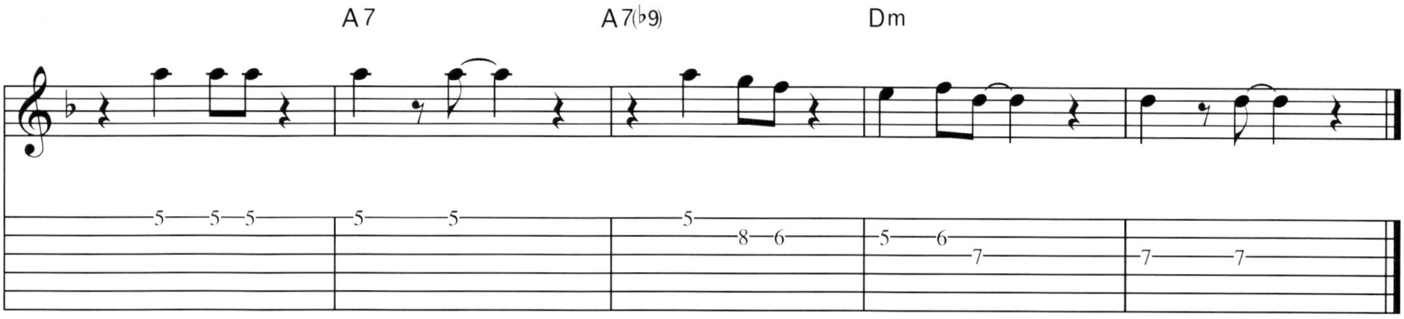

Improvisation tools

1. Use the D harmonic minor scale for the A-parts (Dm, Gm, A7, A7♭9).

2. B part : use G harmonic minor over D7/Gm and the F major scale over C7/F. For A7 apply the chord tones or the harmonic minor scale from the 5th degree (start with A).

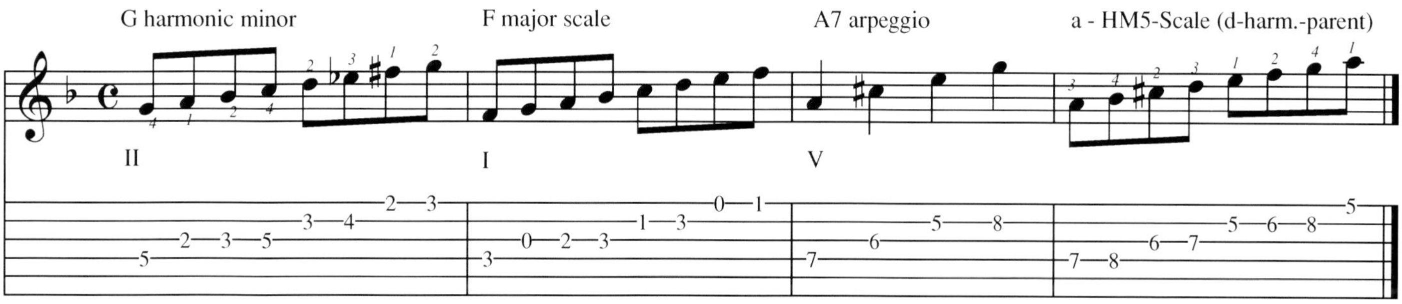

MINOR STOMP (2)

6,16

Felix Schell

The rhythm guitar

A characteristic of gypsy swing jazz is that the drummer is replaced by one or two rhythm guitar players. Most ensembles had even more guitar players. That caused a strong rhythmic basis. You get the typical swing sound by actively pressing and slightly removing your left hand fingers.

1. Play the bass tones of the chords on the first and the third beat and the higher tones on the second and fourth beat to achieve the fast swing.

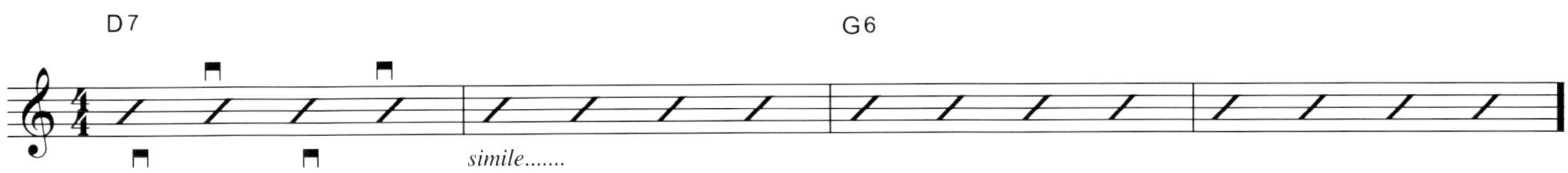

2. For the slow swing, emphasize the first and third beat and play the second and fourth very short.

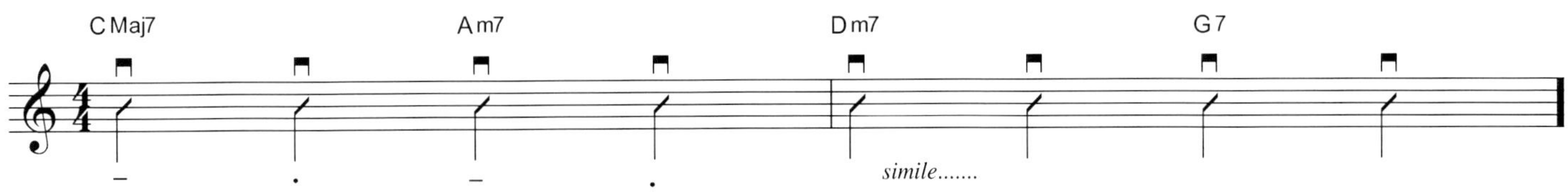

3. For swing waltz, play the bass tones on the first beat and the middle and higher tones on the second and third beat.

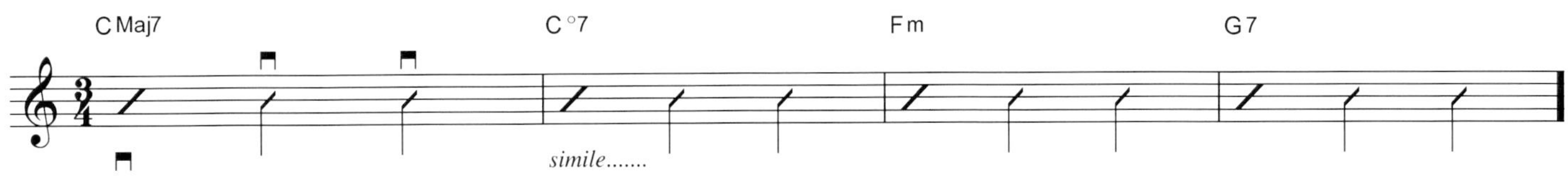

BLUES OF THE GYPSYS

4 bar Intro with diminished arpeggios.
Form: AABBAA
Fast Swing

7,15

Felix Schell

Improvisation tools: A harmonic minor, A blues scale, arpeggios.

CHROMATIC LINE

Medium swing

Form: AABA

Improvisation tools: chords G, Am7, D9 with a G major scale.
Chords Bm7,E9 with an A major scale.
Arpeggio over D♯+, C9 and E♭9.

8,16

Felix Schell

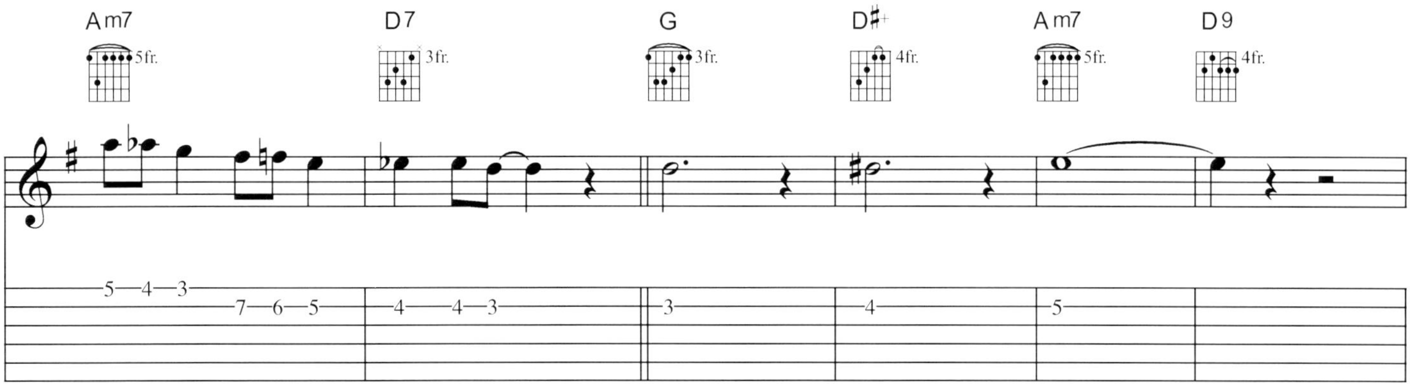

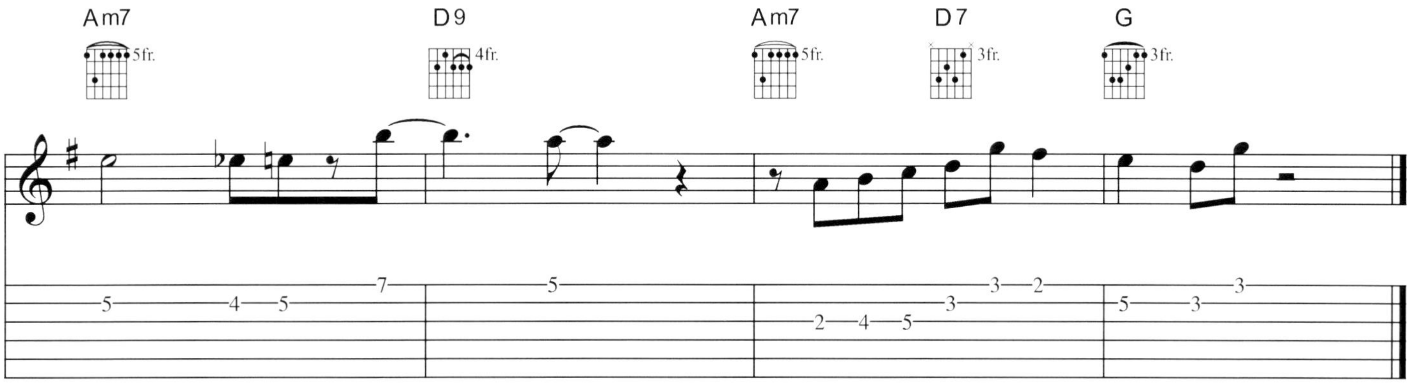

Variations for bar 1-4

1 Bends

#2 completion of chord tones.

#3 flageolet technique:
Make the harmonics by touching the string twelve frets above the fretted note

WALTZ FOR DJANGO

Fast Swing Waltz
Form AABA

9,17

C7
B7
E7
Am6
8fr.
7fr.
5fr.
4fr.
IV
V
D7
G
CMaj7
C°7
3fr.
II
III
Fm
G7
CMaj7
C°7
Fm
G7
CMaj7
C7
F
A♭
D7
G7
C6

LE RÈVE

This piece belongs to the romantic pieces, opposite of the more vigorous solos of hot club swing jazz. Popular pieces are *Nuages* and *Manoir De Mes Rèves* written and performed by Django Reinhardt.

Chords used in this piece:

10

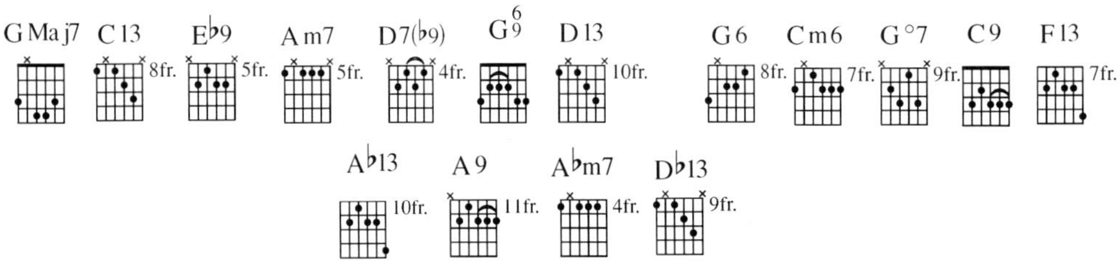

Felix Schell

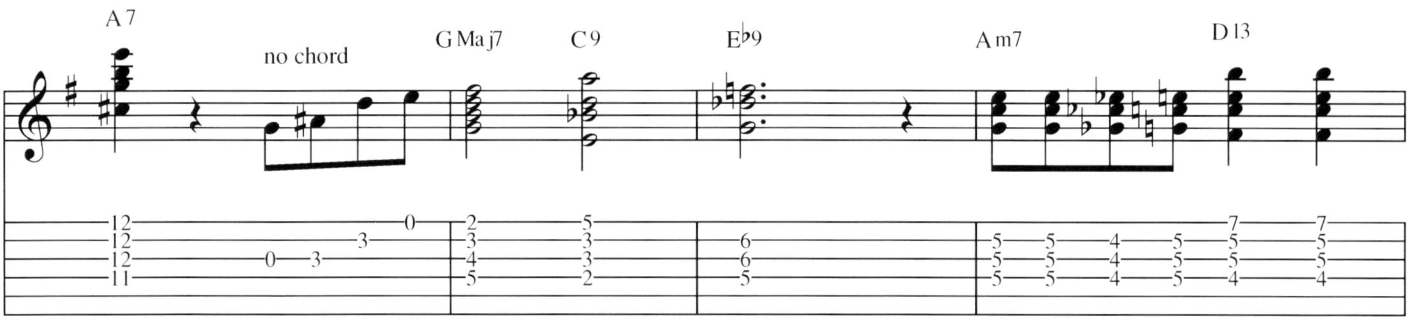

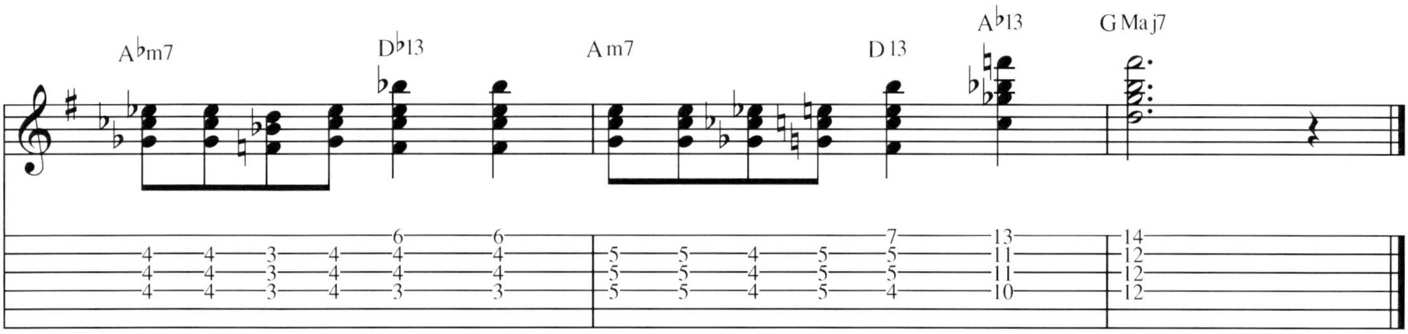

Variations *Le Rève*.
#1 Tremolo

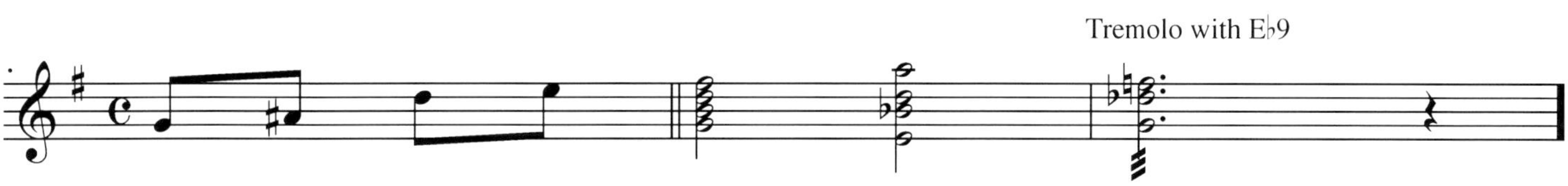

#2 Final harmonic chords on the 12th fret (G6).

DARK EYES

Traditional pieces play an important role in gypsy jazz. In most concerts, the old songs are accompanied by voices. Dark Eyes is a well-known traditional piece in a typical minor mood. The arrangement uses chords and single note lines.

11

Traditional
Arranged: Felix Schell

A7
Dm6
A7
Dm
A7
Dm
Gm
Dm
A7
Dm6

Improvisation.

The skill of using improvisation tools has to be practiced. Most important is the knowledge of arpeggios. These are chords played tone after tone. There are many books that deal with the theme of arpeggios. Major and minor scales are important too, as the symmetrical scales. These consist of similar steps: the chromatic scale, the whole tone scale and the so called gypsy scale, built of minor thirds.

On one side, there's the knowledge, one the other, there's the practice. There are many musicians, who are used to the scales, but who are not capable of improvising. If you start improvising, always look for an easy way. Think of different musical themes that you could play to the chord changes. The following examples may help you.

The A-part of *One note rhythm* is built of a repetition of a 2 bar Cadenza (Anatol, Turnaround.) Think of different ways of improvising over these 8 bars.

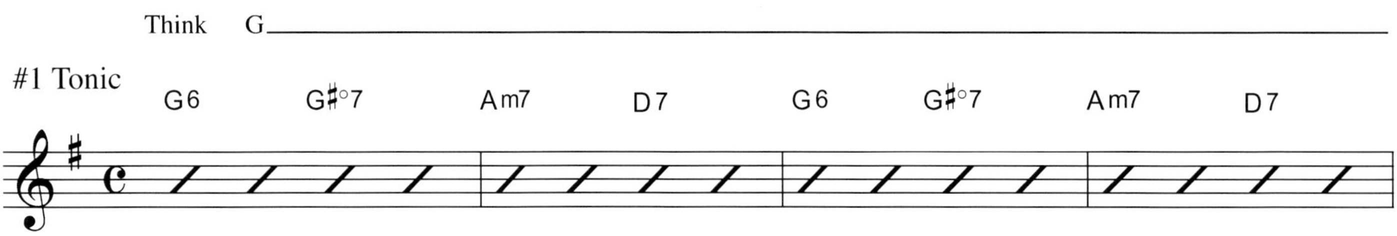

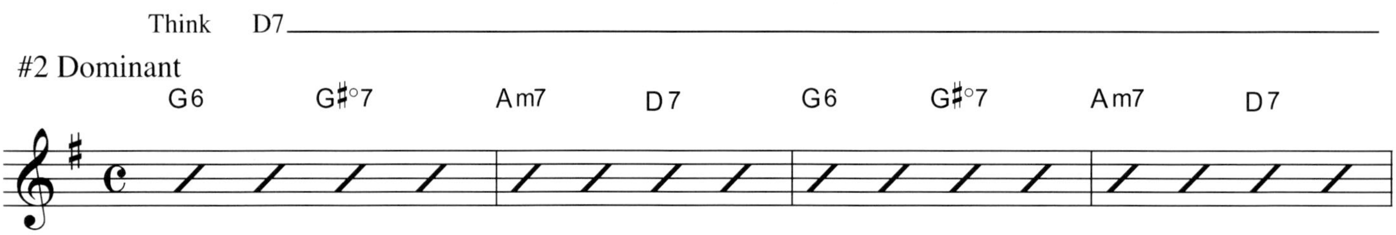

PATTERN #1:
Use the tones of the G6 chord.

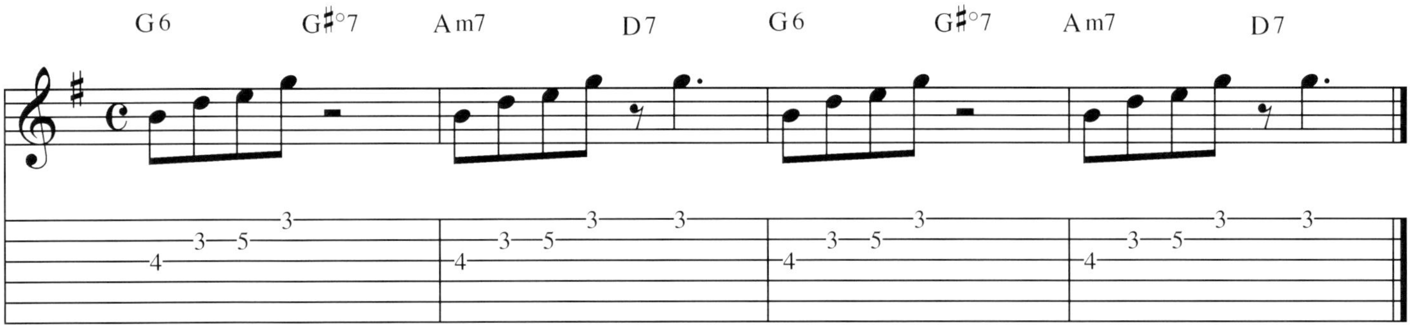

PATTERN #2:
#3 Use the tones of the D7 chord.

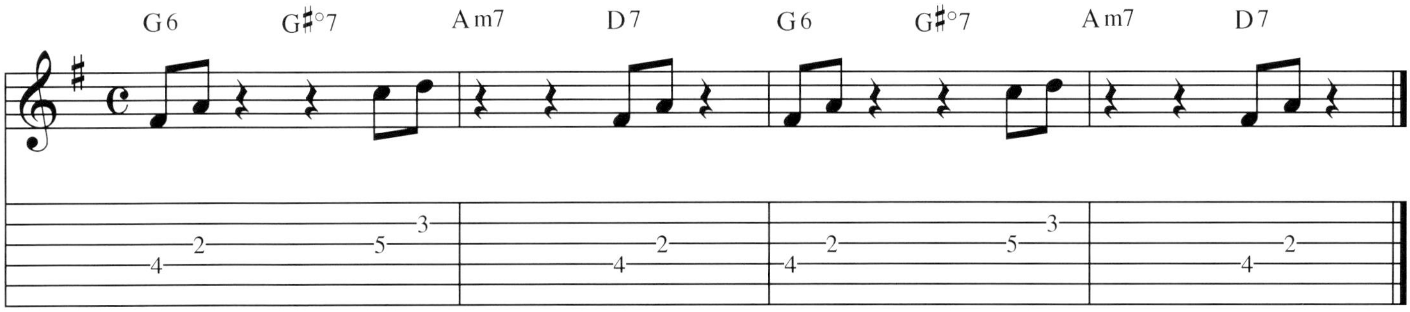

PATTERN #3:
#3 Use the tones of the G♯°7 (diminshed 7) chord.

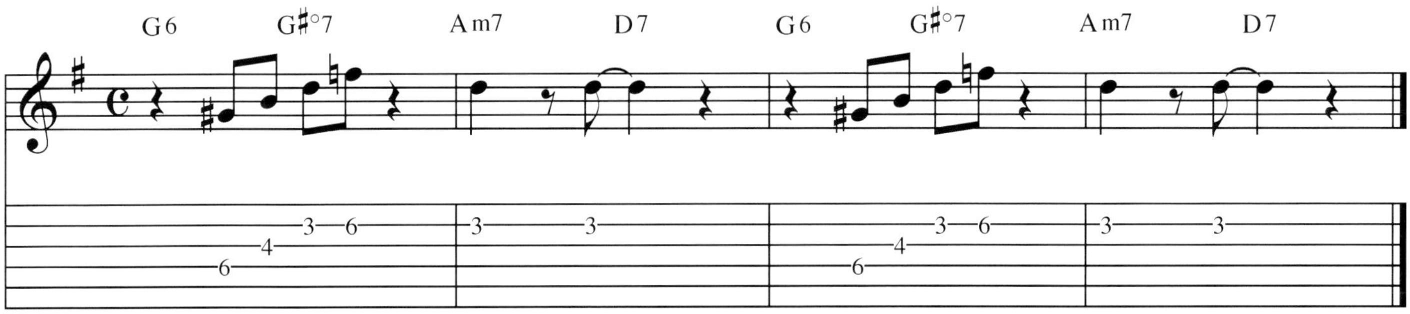

PATTERN #4 (gemischt):
#3 Use the tones of the G6 and the D7 chord.

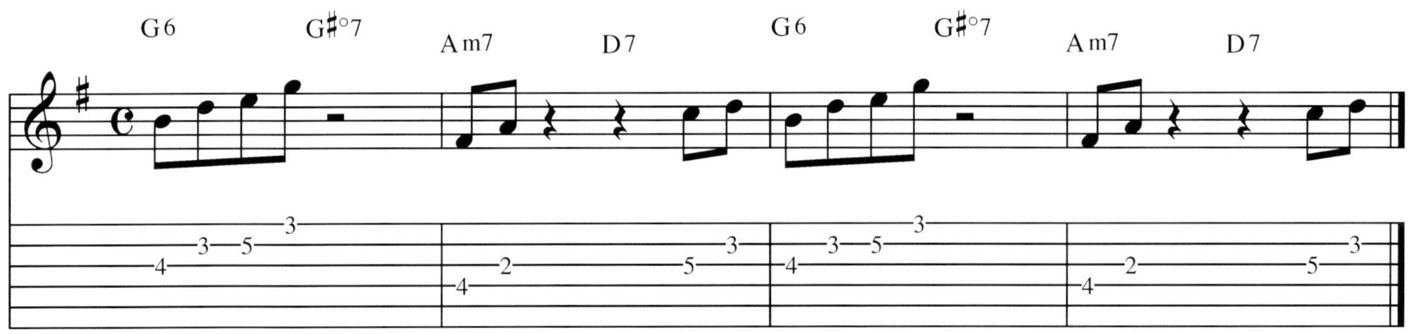

SPECIAL EFFECTS

The guitar is a popular instrument, not only because of it's specific sound, but also for the possibility of creating special sounding effects. Advanced players create sound effects to play their songs in a most interesting way.

#5 Glissando

The glissando is a sliding movement from one pitch to another on the same string. It is indicated by a line, drawn between two note heads.

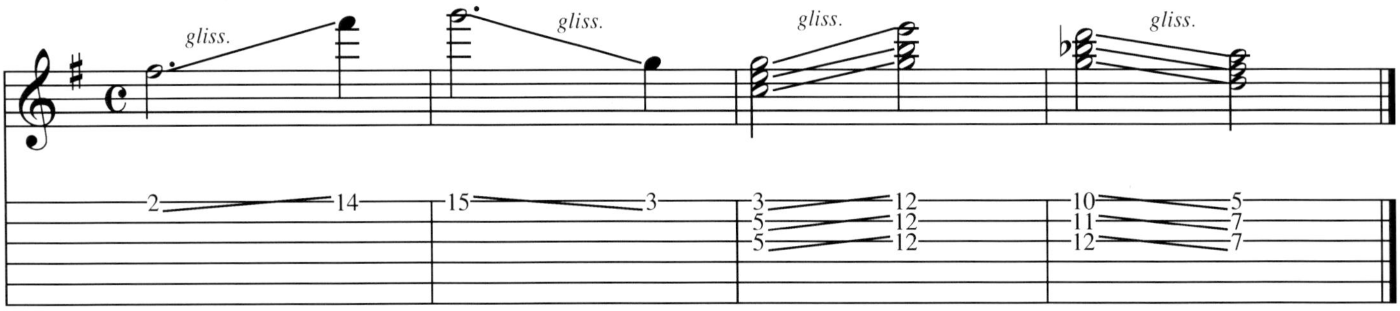

#6 Tremolo

The tremolo is a fast and repeated (detached) attack of an individual pitch, double-stop, or chord.
A combination of tremolo and glissando is possible.

#7 Chromatics

Chromatic approaches can come from any tone above or below the melody note. The length of the chromatic line can be as long or short as desired. It is important to know which note is the melody note.

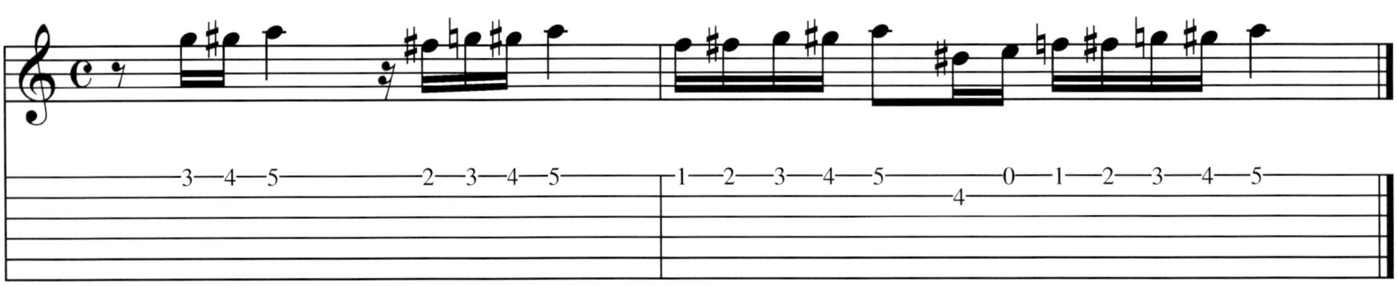

#8 The Hammer-on and Pull-off technique

This does not require a pick. It creates a fluid motion between two or more notes that can last for as long as the player desires. The Hammer-on uses the force of the finger (of the fretboard hand) hitting the string to sound the note, similar to a piano hammer.
The Pull-off, is used for descending to another pitch usually a half or a whole tone step.

#9 Octave techniques
The first finger plays the G string, the 4th finger the upper E string (2nd and 3rd fingers to not touch the strings.) So that we can stroke the plectrum (or thumb) across the G to the E string, we have to muffle the B string. This is done by the 1st finger, so that the underside of the finger touches the B string and muffles it.

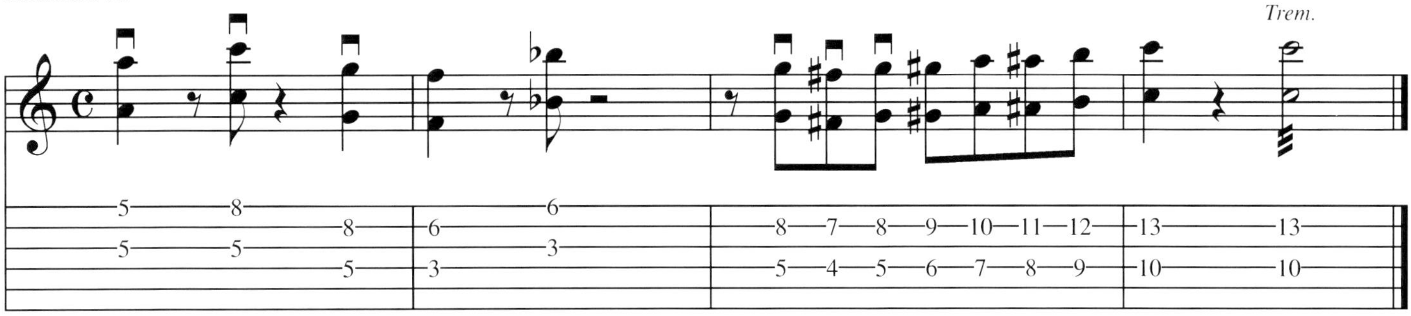

#10 Harmonics
The guitar is able to produce harmonics very effectively. Natural harmonics are found on the 5th, 7th and 12th fret.

#11 Bends
The bending technique is used to raise the pitch of a note creating an effect similar to a short glissando. The bend requires a finger to be placed in the position of the fretted note, then to push or pull the string, which increases the tension and raises the pitch of the fretted note.

#12 Bend Release
Place a finger on the indicated note and bend the string a full (or half) step without picking. Strike the string and release the bend back to the written note.

#13 Slide up
Slide from one or two frets below up to the indicated note.

#14 Slide down
Slide from one or two frets above down to the written note.

#15 Legato, Tenuto and Staccato
Legato: keep fingers to fretboard for a long sounding.
Tenuto: long, soft sounding
Staccato: short sounding

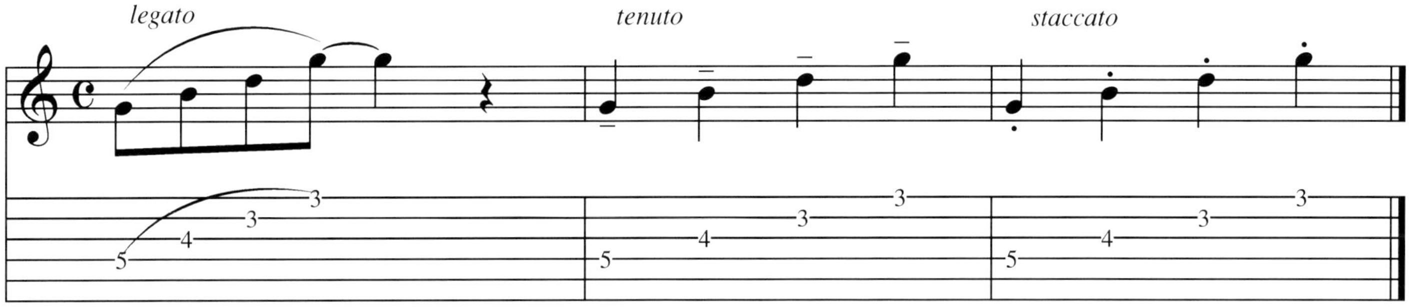

ARPEGGIOS

The fingerings of the arpeggios are as movable as the chords on the fretboard.

#15 Arpeggios with the root on the 6th string (E)

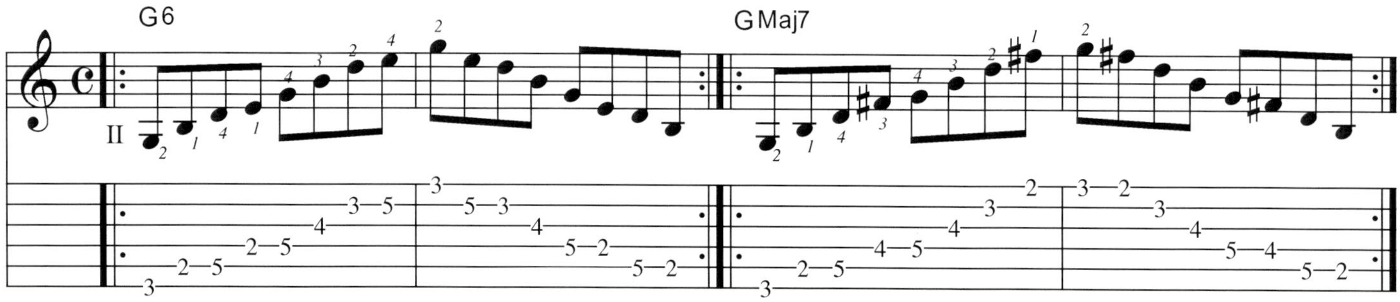

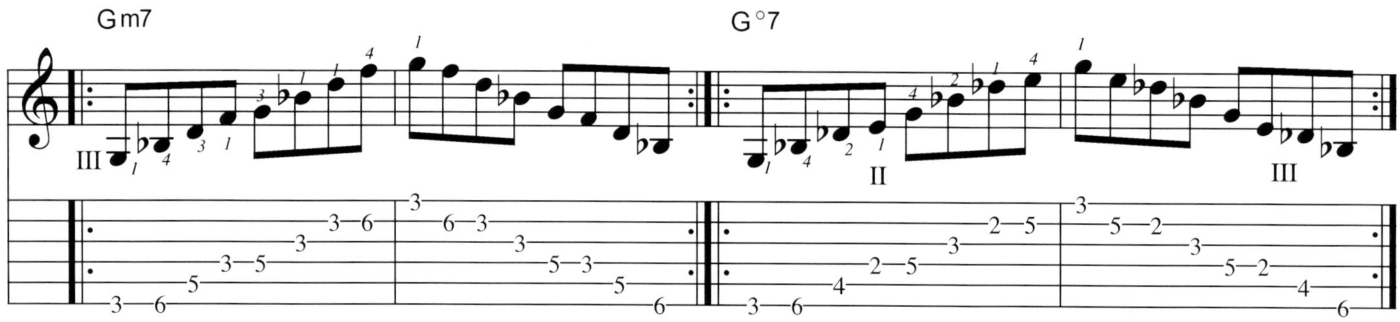

#16 Arpeggios with the root on the 5th string (A)

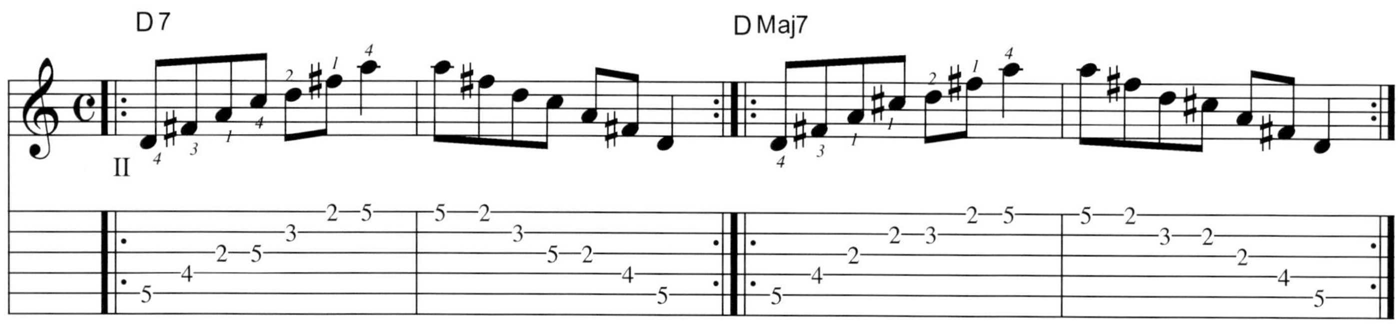

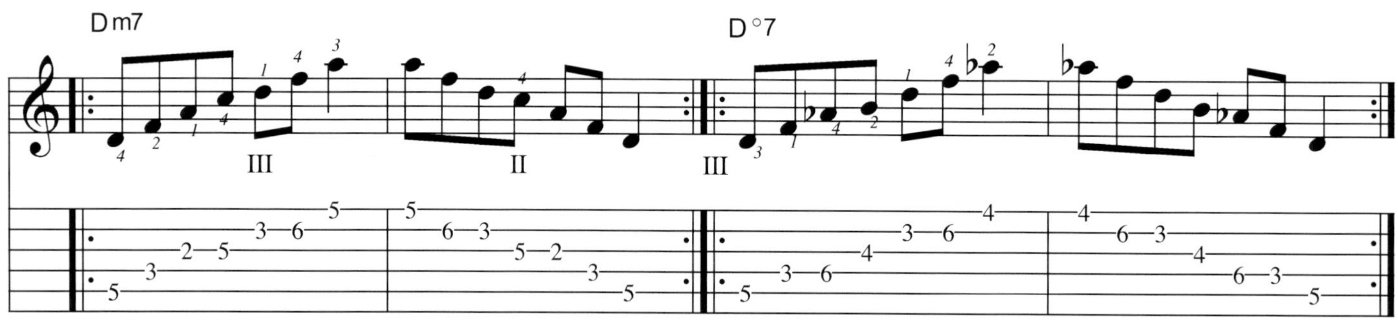

#17 Arpeggios with the root on the 4th string (D)

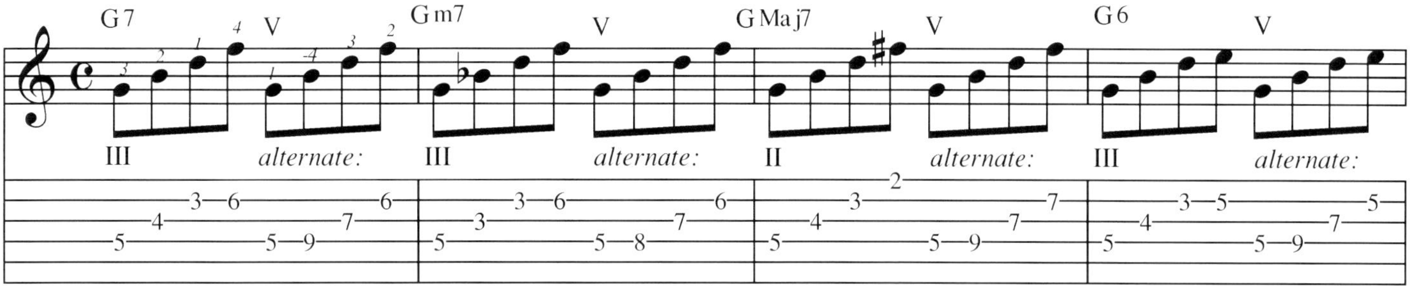

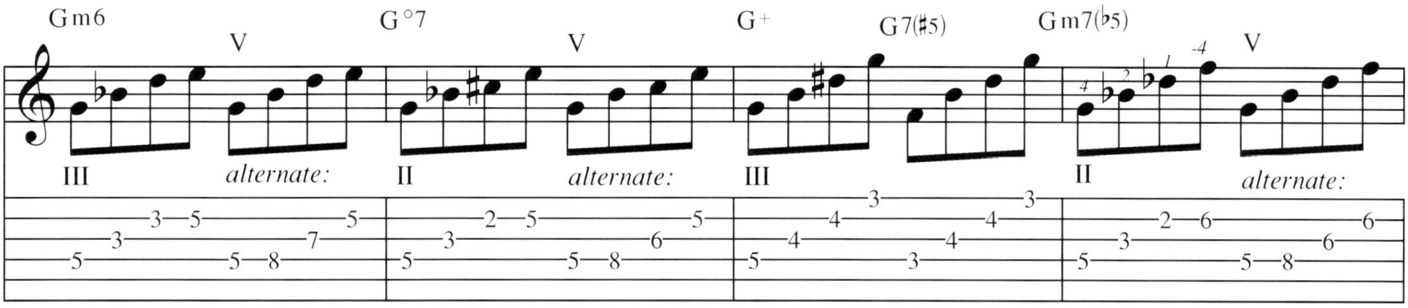

SCALES.

#18 Major scales

These "closed" fingerings may be shifted up the fretboard for transposition.

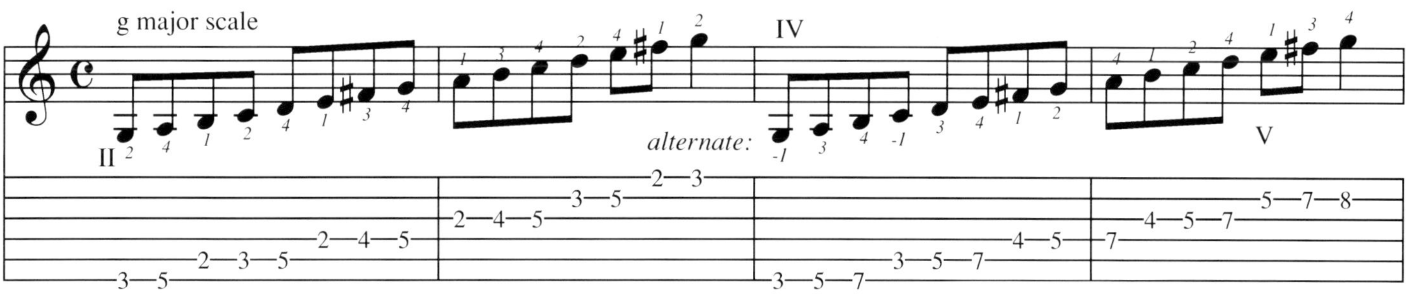

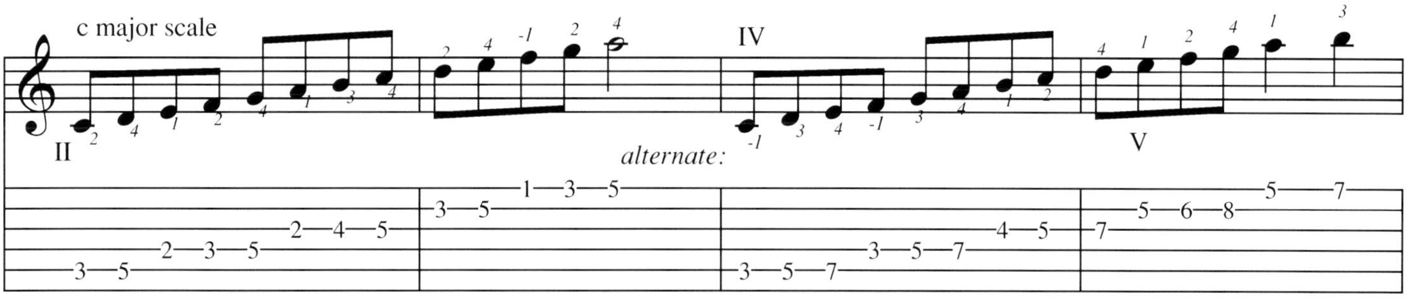

You can use the G major scale with the following chords: G6 (or Maj7), Am7, Bm7, CMaj7, D7, Em7 and F♯m7(♭5).

You can use the C major scale with the following chords: C6 (or Maj7), Dm7, Em7, FMaj7, G7, Am7 and Bm7(♭5).

MINOR SCALES
#19 harmonic minor

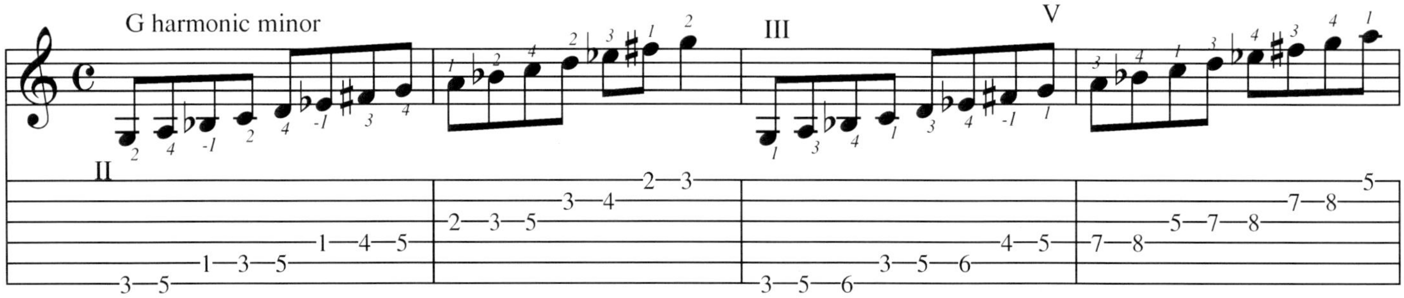

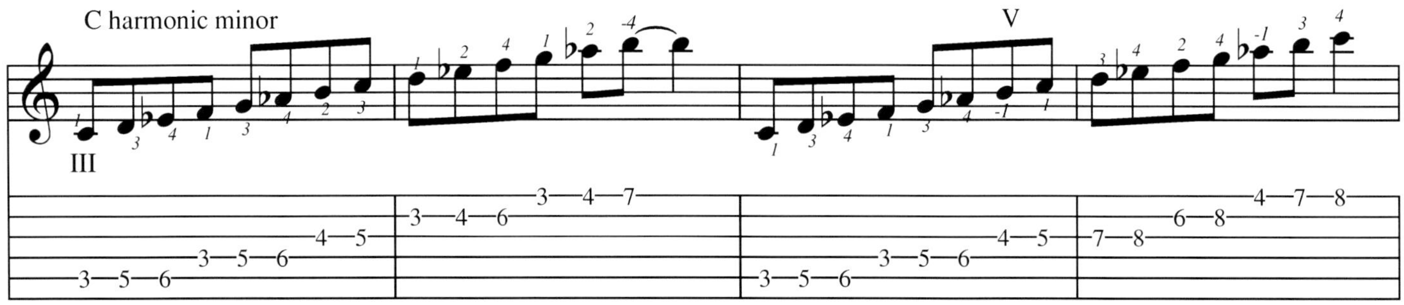

You can use the G harmonic minor scale with the following chords: Gm, Cm and D7, C7(♭9), D7(♯9)
You can use the C harmonic minor scale with the following chords: Cm, Fm and C7, C7(♭9), C7(♯9)

#20: Melodic Minor

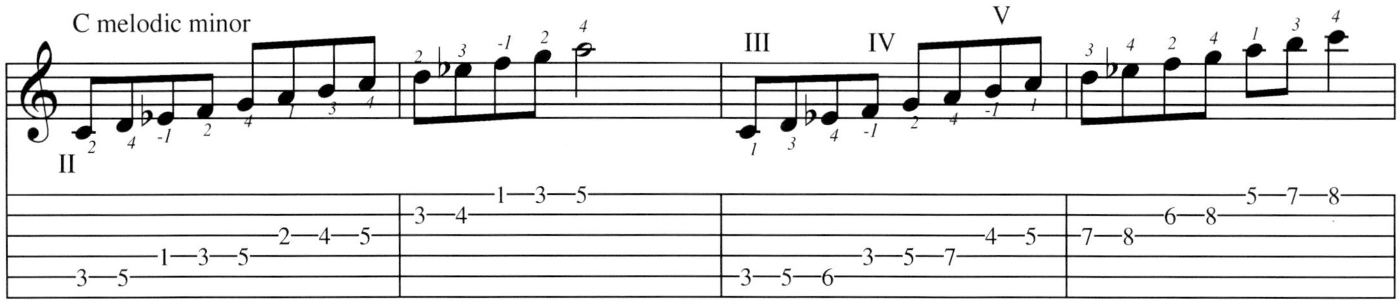

You can use the G melodic minor scale with the following chords: Gm, C, D7, D7(♭9)
You can use the C melodic minor scale with the following chords: Cm, F, G7, G7(♭9)

SYMETRICAL SCALES

#21. Chromatic Scale:

Combine the chromatic scale with the dominant or an arpeggio.
Pseudo-symmetrical scale: G is the basis and every interval is played in a chromatic way.

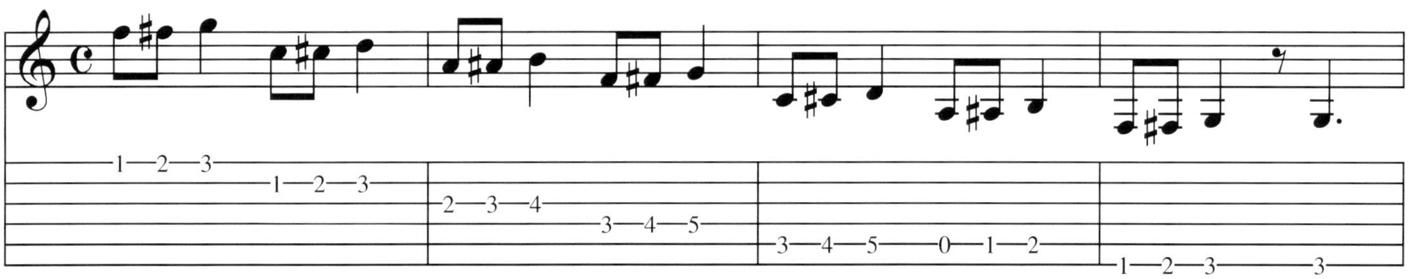

#22 Whole tone scale with 7♯5 chords.

The whole tone scale can be played with the dominant.

Pseudo-symmetrical scale: D7 Arpeggio with whole tones approaching the interval steps.

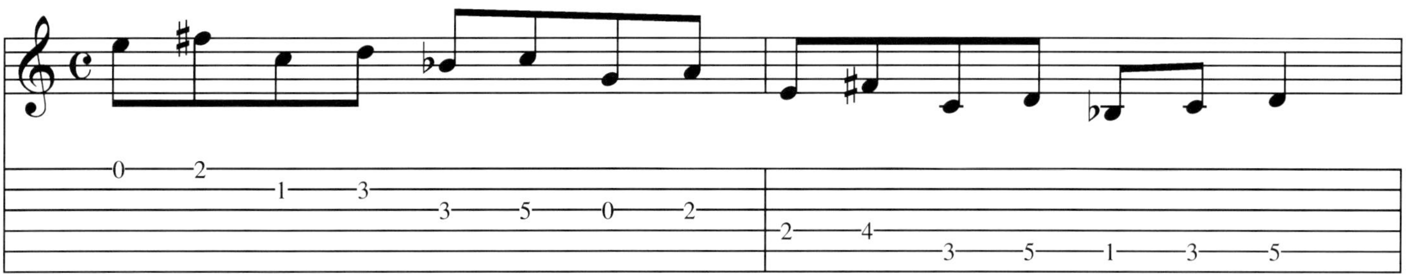

MELODIC EMBELISHMNTS.

Melodic embellishment
Example : "Brother John"
#1 Slide, Hammer On, Pull Off.

About the Author

Felix Schell was born on June 25, 1951, in Mainz, Germany. He has played guitar since the age of 13. For many years he played rock n' roll, blues, and jazz in different bands. After studying music at the Jazzschool München, he taught jazz guitar there for three years. Felix also played with the Musical Hair Ensemble in the '70s. Today, Felix Schell is the author of several instruction books, as well as the owner of a publication and distribution service in Hamburg, Germany.